The Ultimate Recreation Center Makeover

An Exciting Experience at William Walker Recreation Center

A Collaboration by the amazing kids that attend William Walker Recreation Center

3G Publishing, Inc.
Loganville, Ga 30052
www.3gpublishinginc.com
Phone: 1-888-442-9637

©2024 City of Atlanta. All rights reserved.

No part of this book may be reproduced, stored in a retrieval system, or transmitted by any means without the written permission of the author.

First published by 3G Publishing, Inc. August, 2024.

ISBN:

Printed in the United States of America

Because of the dynamic nature of the Internet, any web addresses or links contained in this book may have changed since publication and may no longer be valid. The views expressed in this work are solely those of the author and do not necessarily reflect the views of the publisher, and the publisher hereby disclaims any responsibility for them.

Introduction

Welcome to William Walker Recreation Center! In the heart of our city lies a place where dreams take flight and adventures come to life. This is a very special recreation center; it's where curious and fearless young minds are taking a journey to explore what their true passions are. Join us on a journey filled with dreams, hope and great memories. Are you ready to see what a great mind your chilld has? Let's step into William Walker Recreation Center where the extraordinary becomes ordinary, and the impossible is just another fun challenge under the supervision of Coach Mike and the William Walker staff!

Coach Mike is a passionate and dedicated instructor who inspires his students to excel both academically and personally. He consistently encourages critical thinking and empowers students to think outside the box. With a creative teaching style and a knack for making lessons engaging, he brings out the best in his students, allowing them to discover their full potential.

Spending time with Coach Mike was the best fun the kids would have all week. They ran relay races, played spelling games, won prizes, and learned to have an imagination to design their boring recreation room.

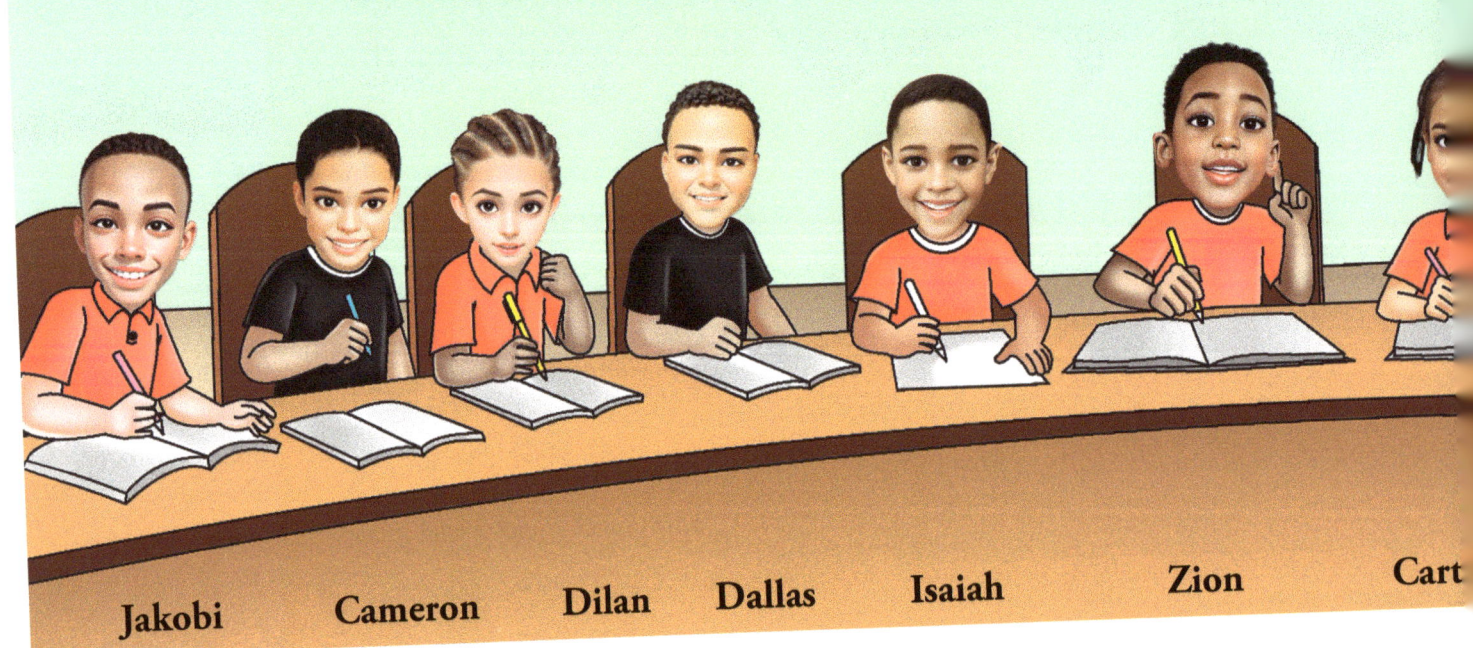

Jakobi Cameron Dilan Dallas Isaiah Zion Cart

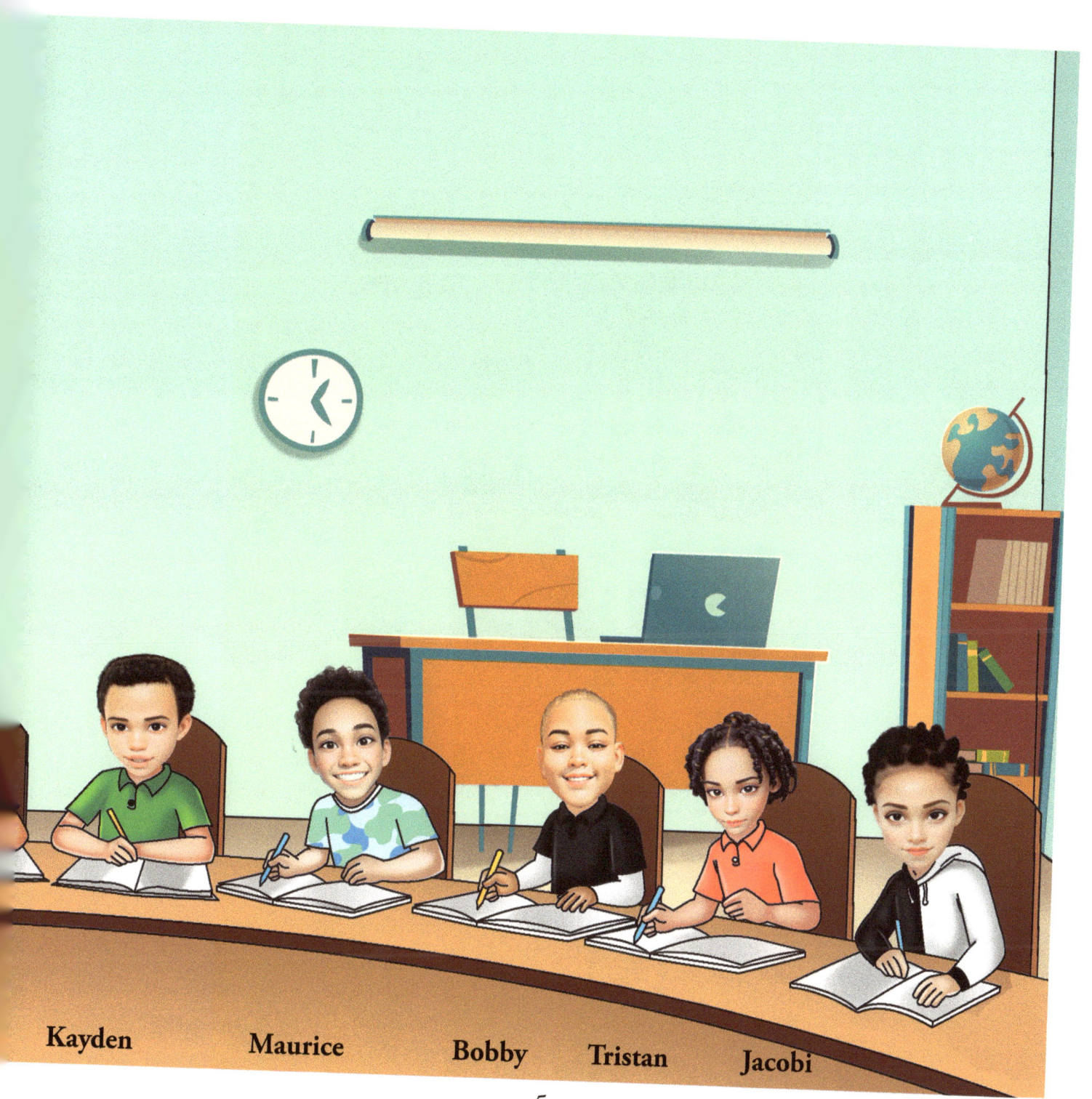

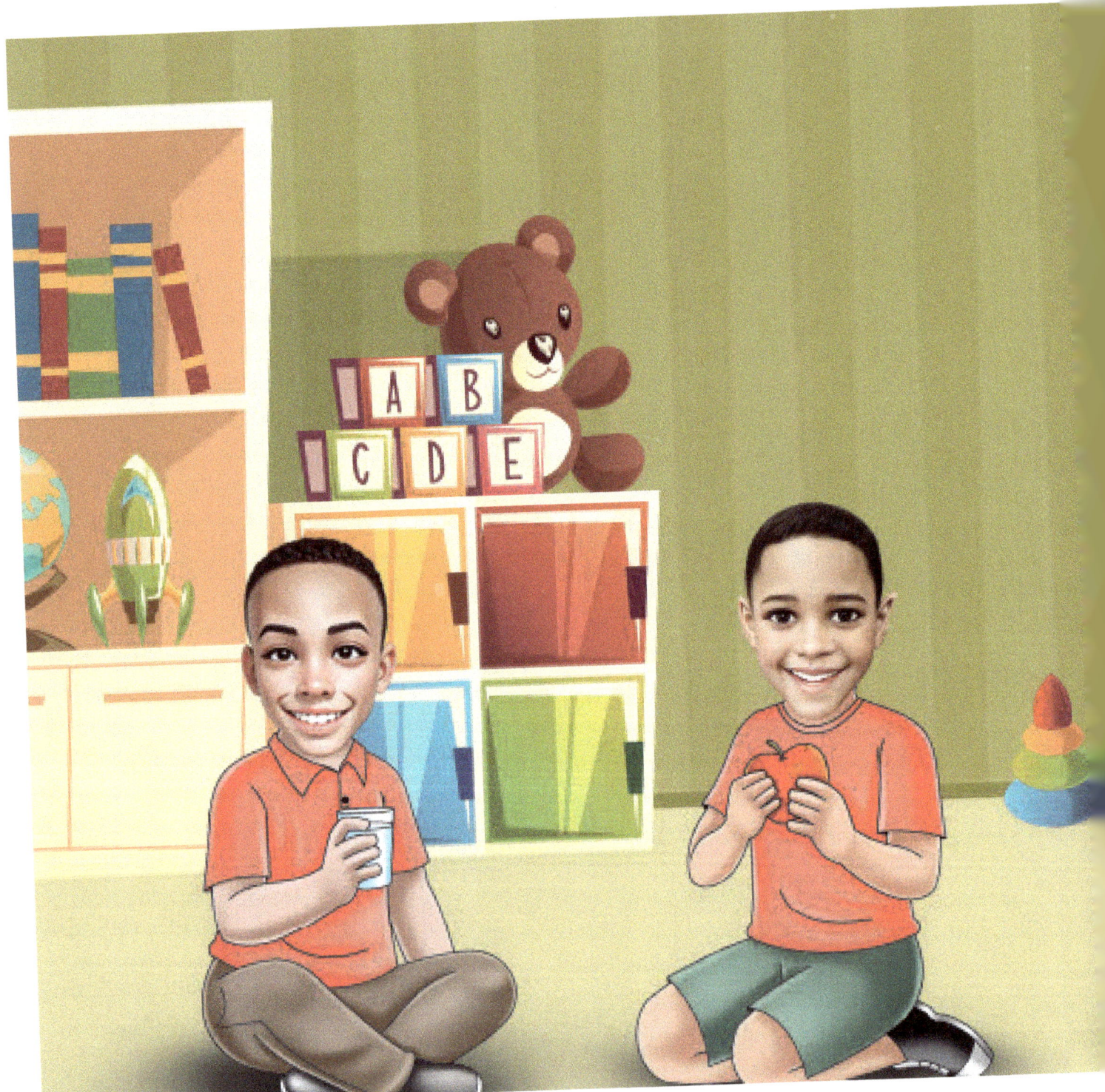

We had so much fun planning the decorating of our Recreation Center. Everyone got a chance to tell Coach Mike what they wanted to do in their space to have fun.

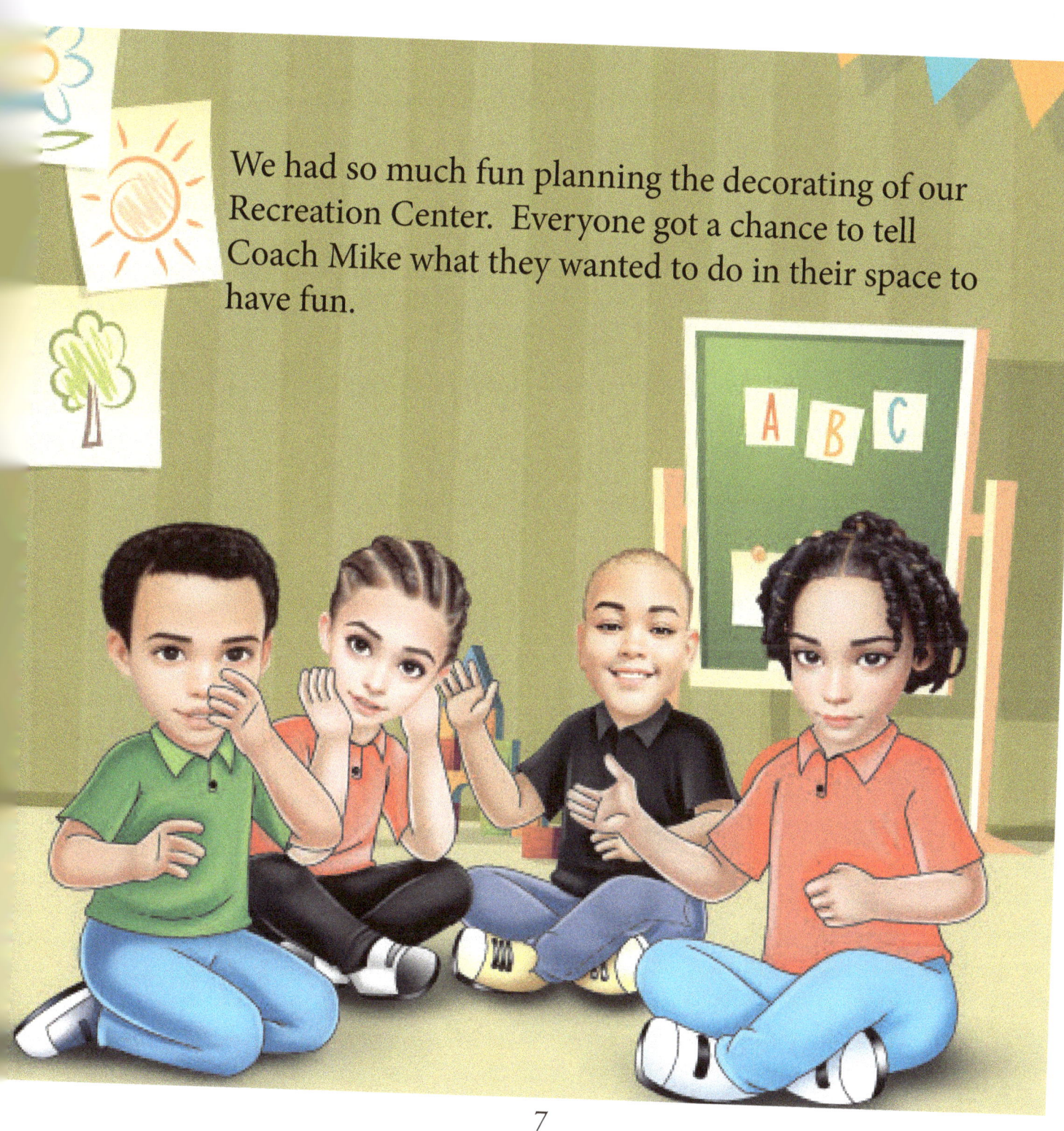

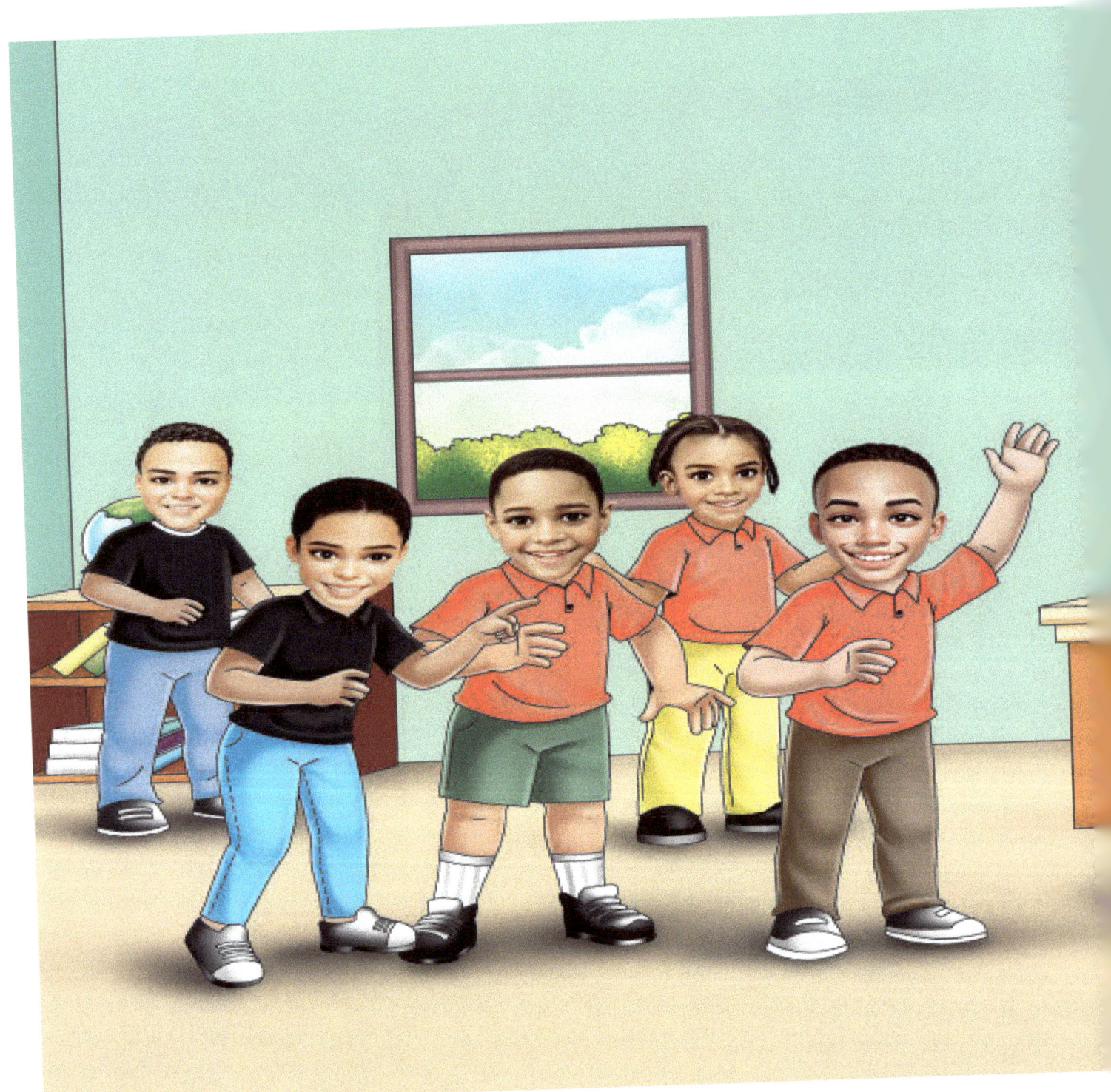

Coach Mike helped us make our design of the new recreation center, and we were all excited to see it on paper.

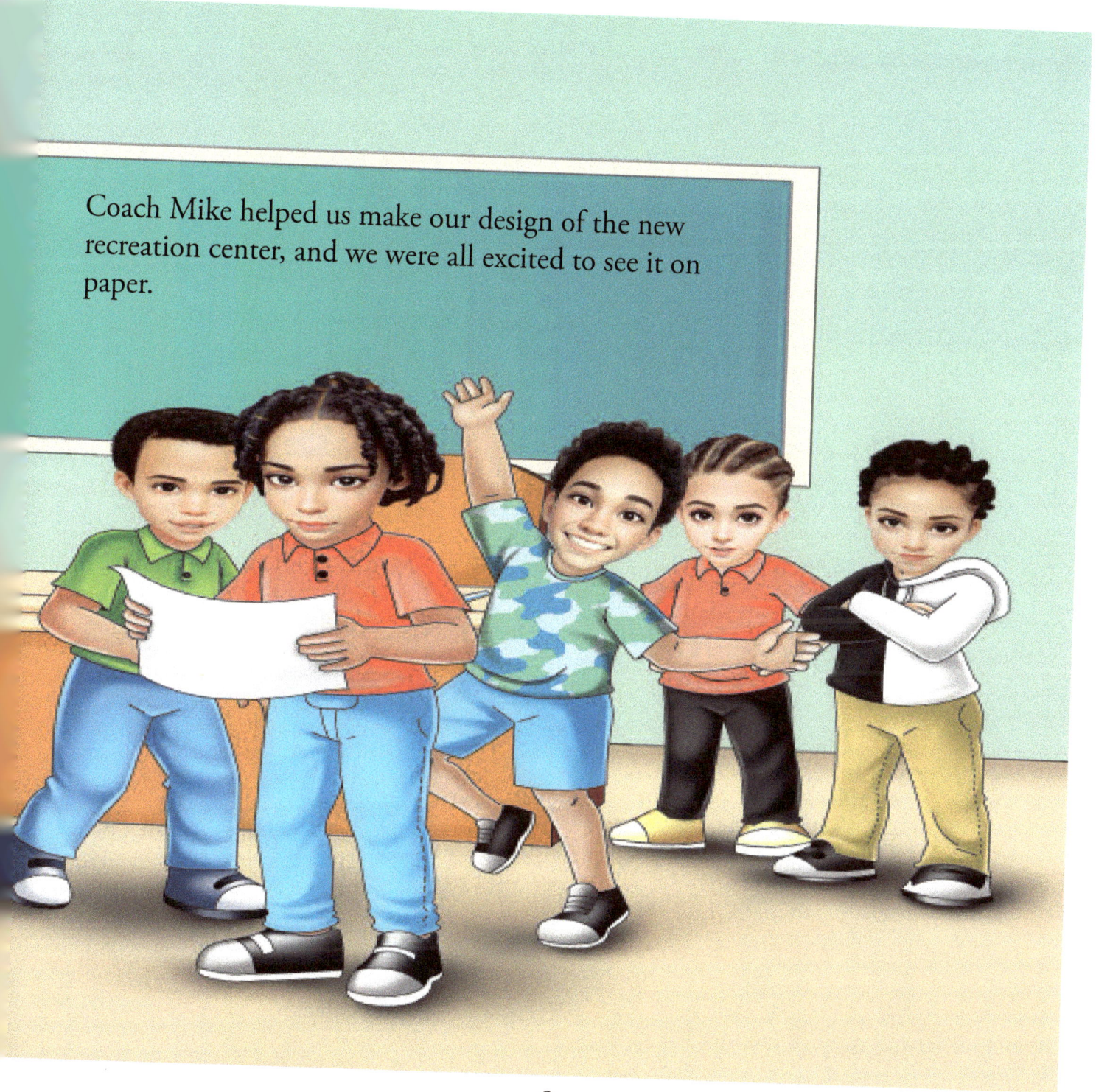

We all decided to go have some snacks in our new snack section, which we had completely designed first. We really needed a snack before we start getting the list together for the supplies we would need to complete our gaming room.

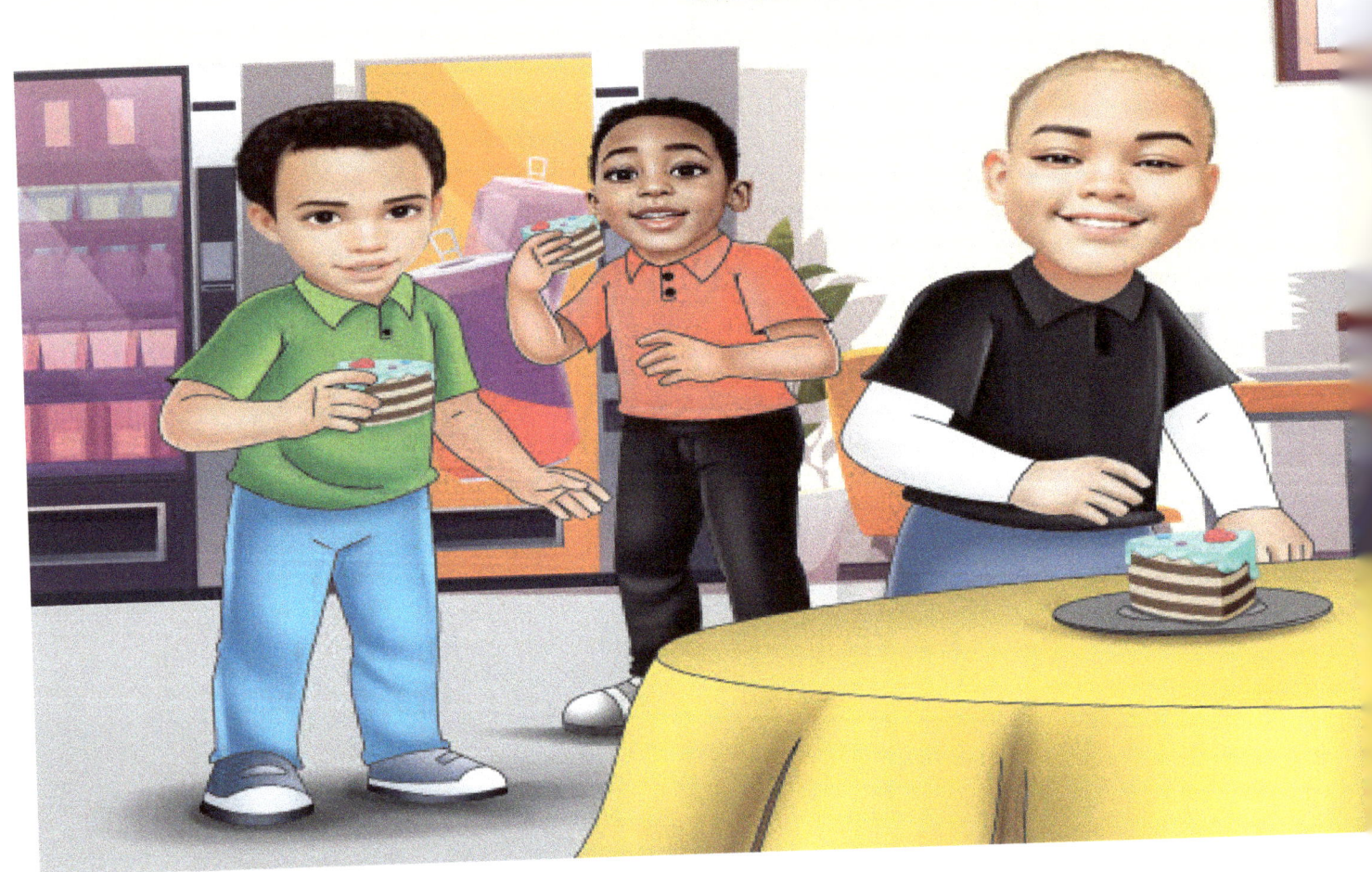

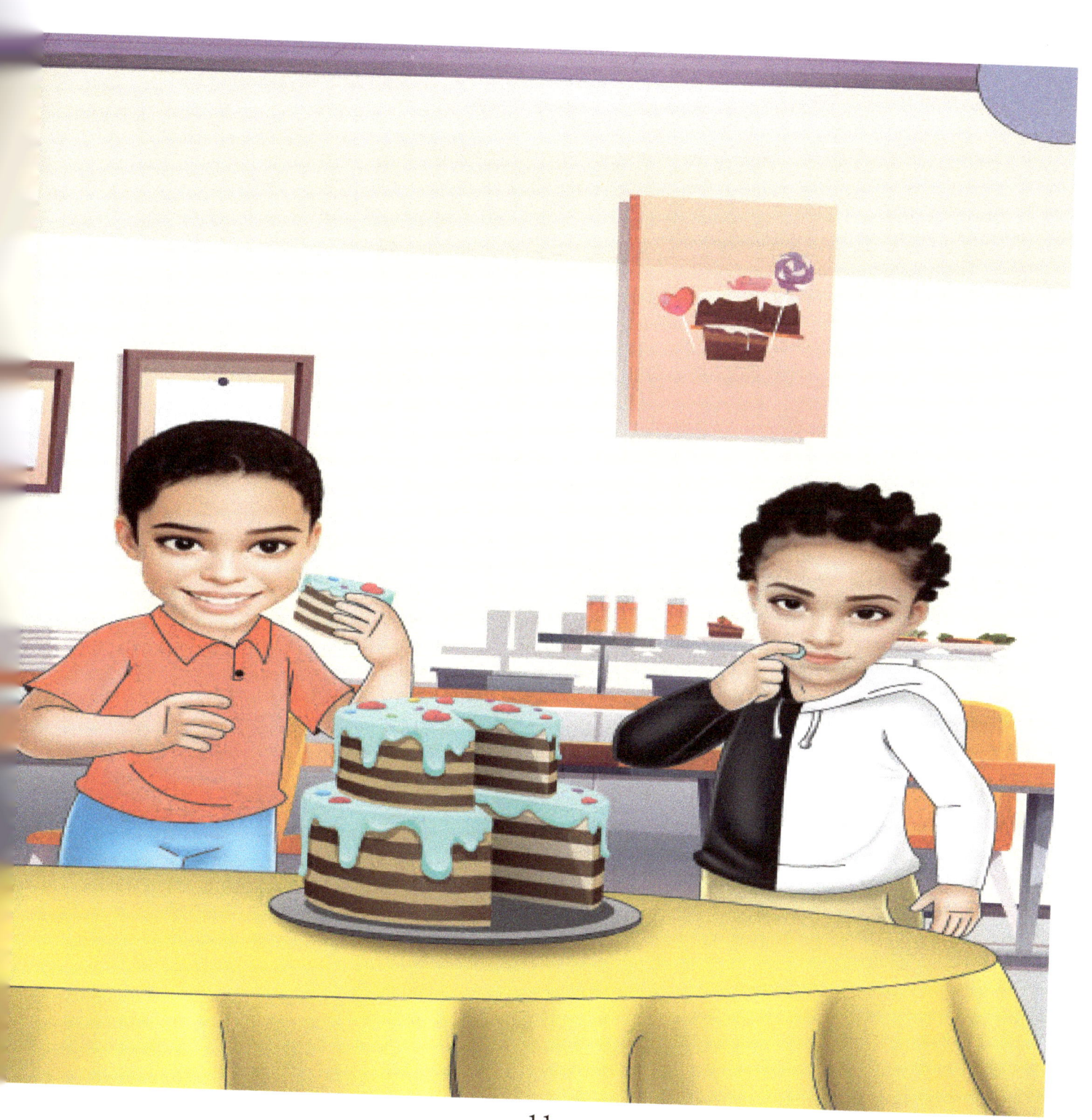

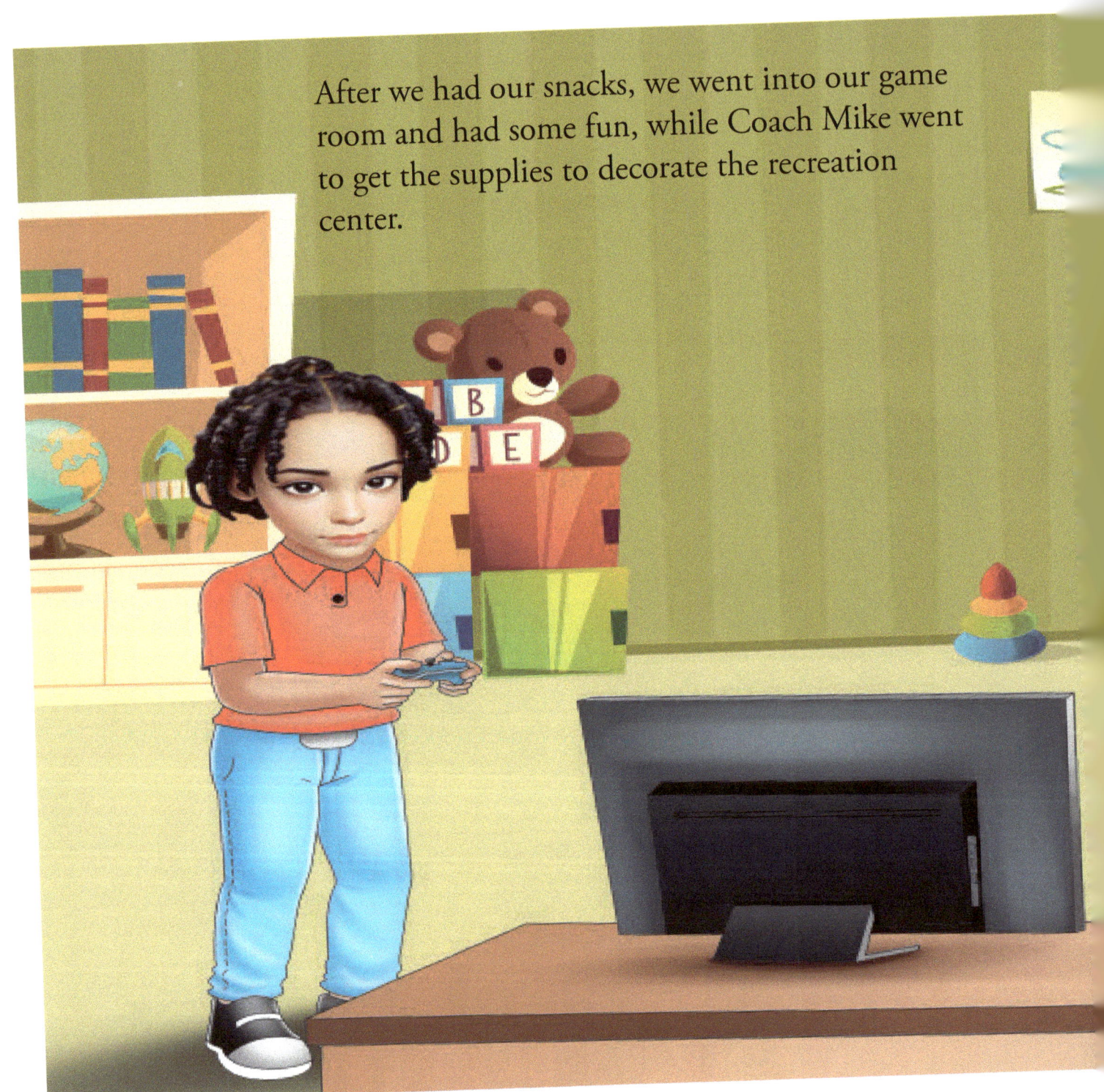

After we had our snacks, we went into our game room and had some fun, while Coach Mike went to get the supplies to decorate the recreation center.

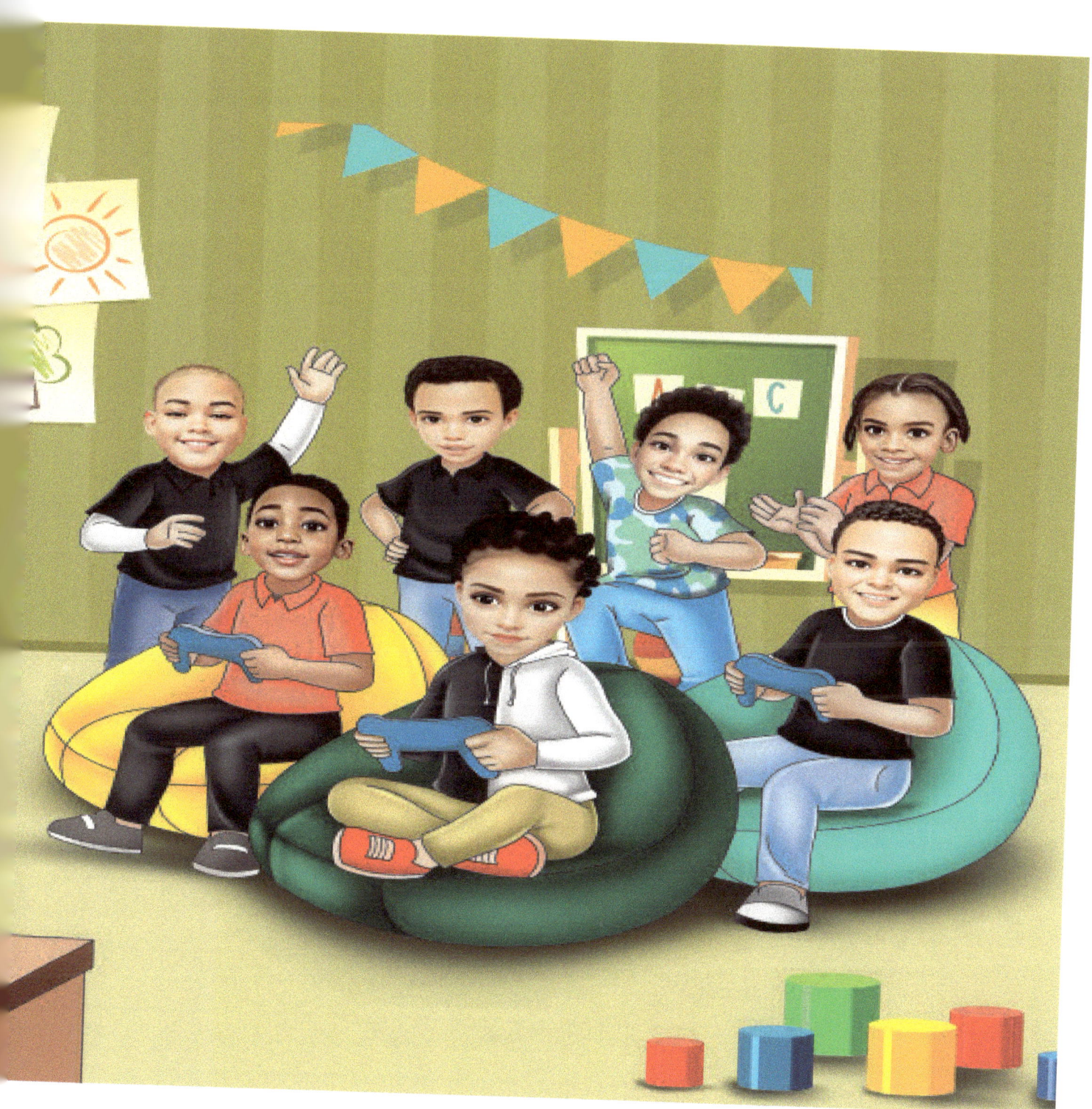

We all promised Coach Mike that we would do our homework before he got back so that we would all be able to work together on painting the room.

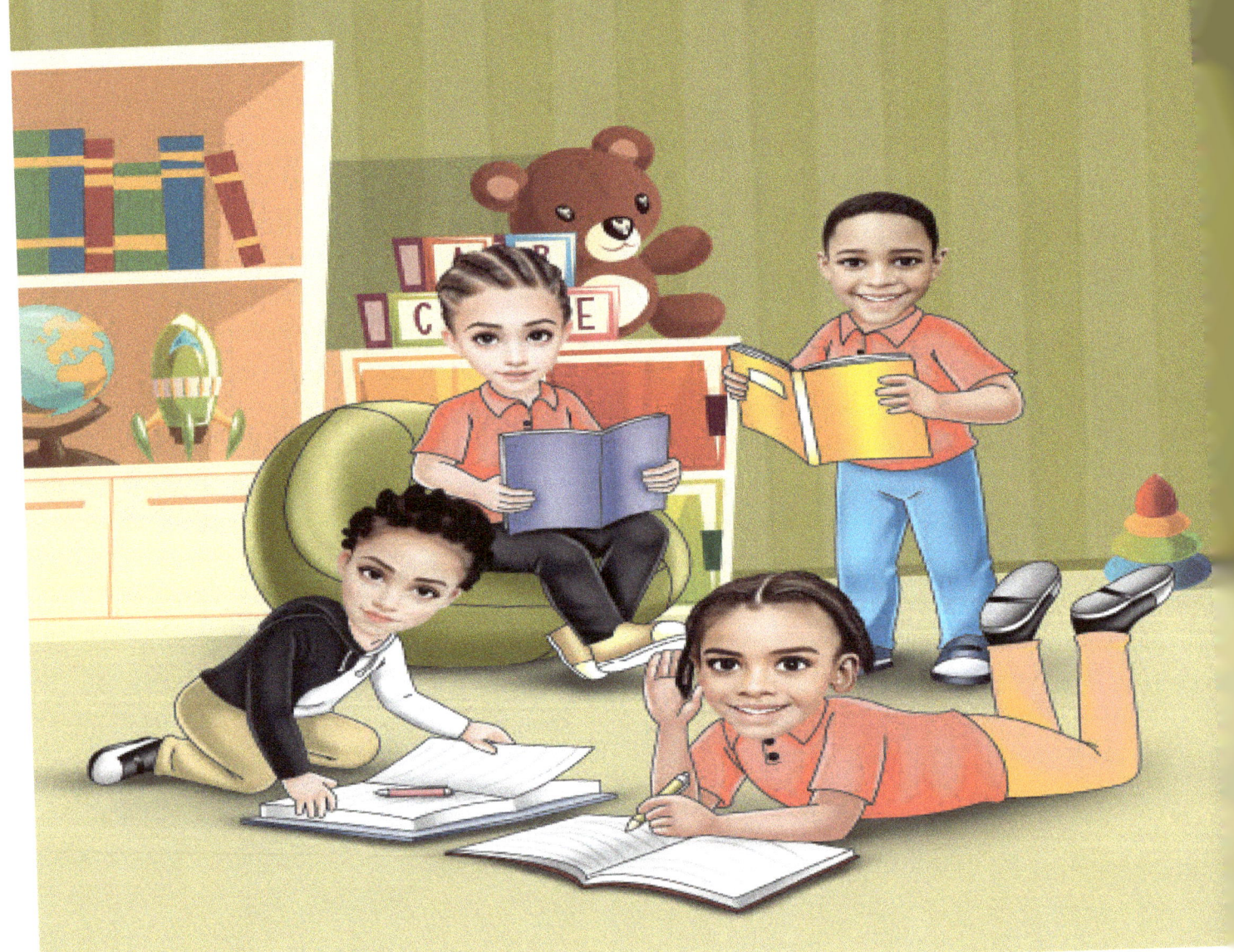

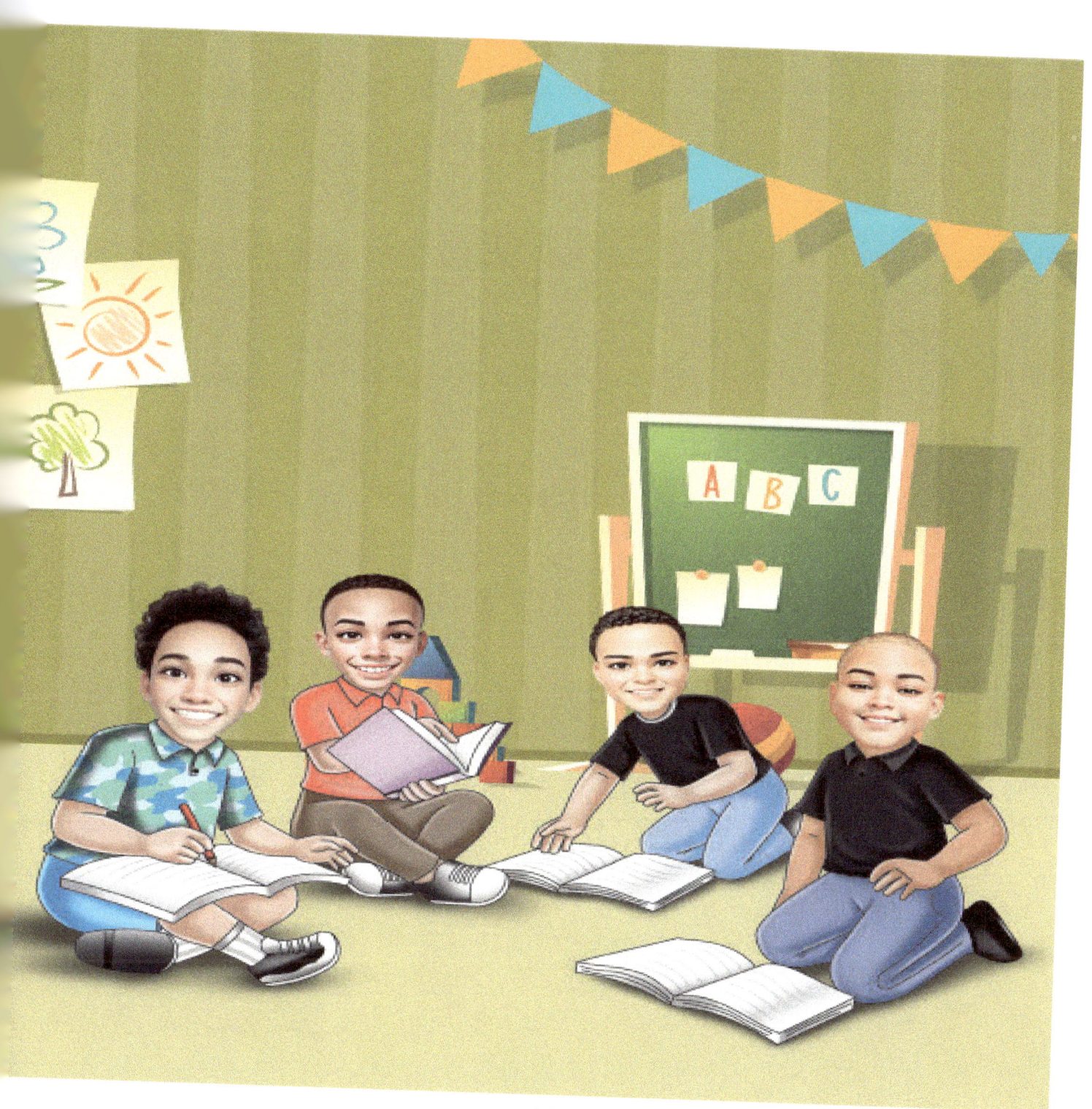

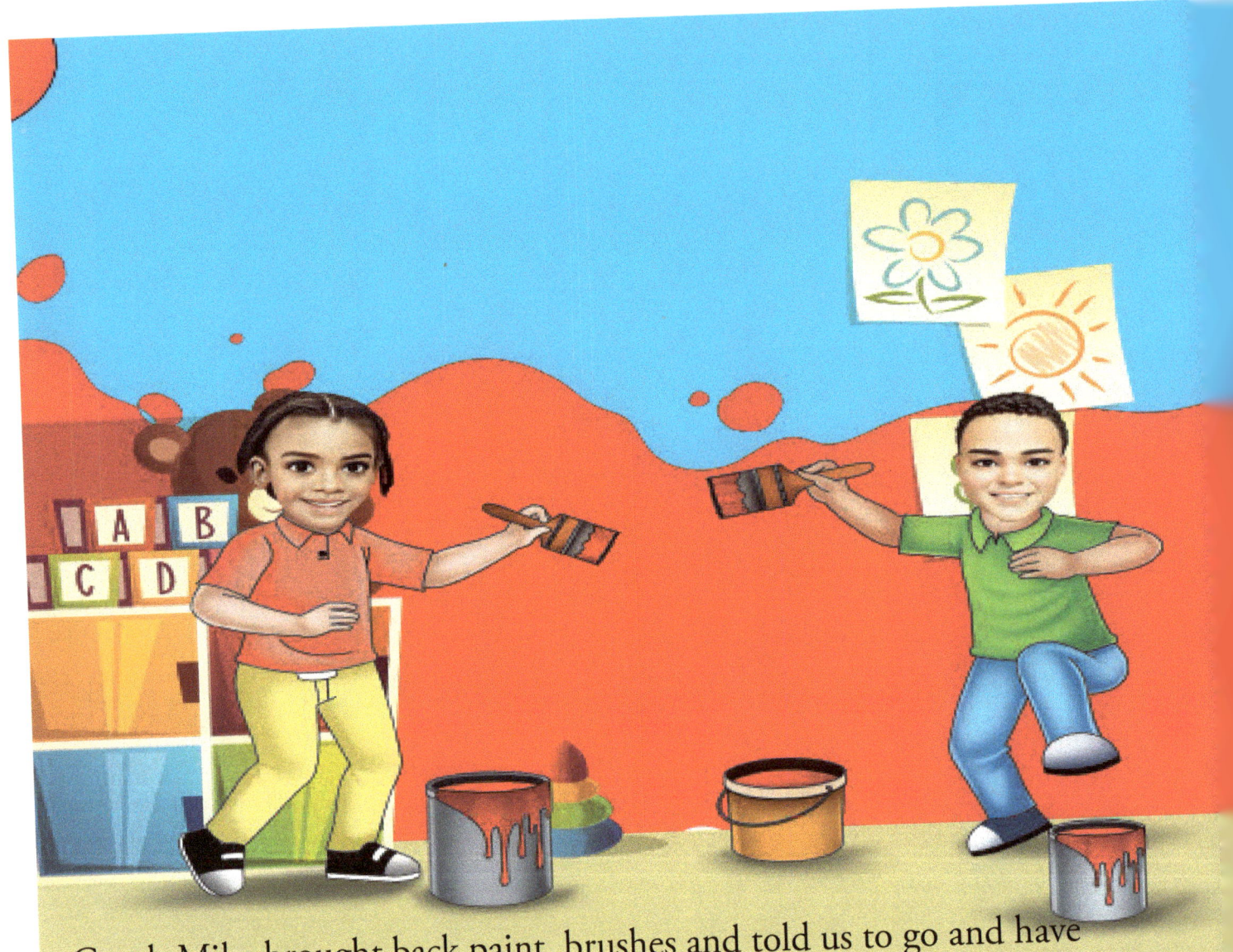

Coach Mike brought back paint, brushes and told us to go and have fun decorating our room, because we did all we were asked to do while he was gone. We are so excited to start painting and decorating!

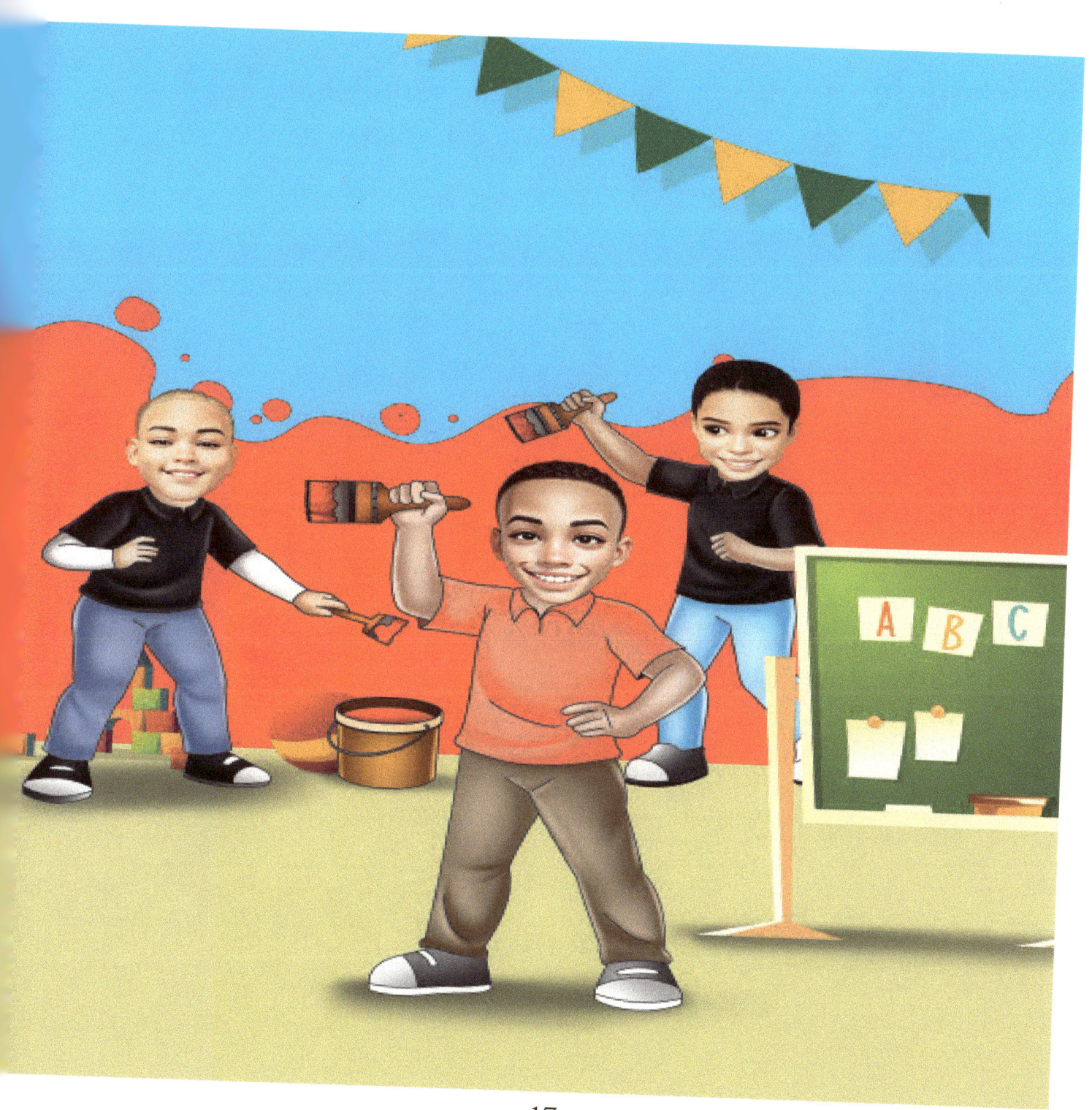

Wow, we got finished, and all the work we did looked amazing. Coach Mike was so proud of us that he gave us all kinds of sports equipment.

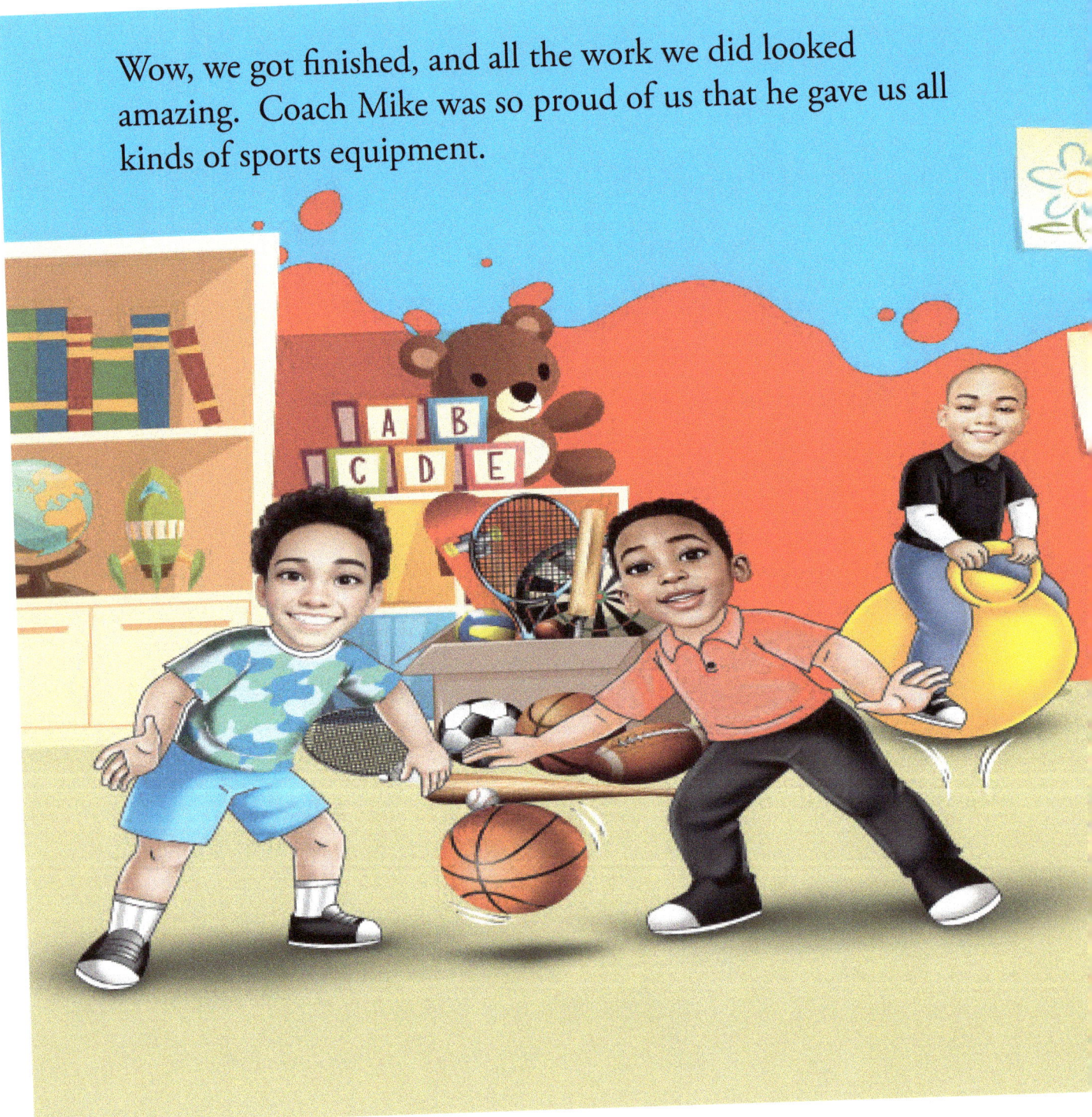

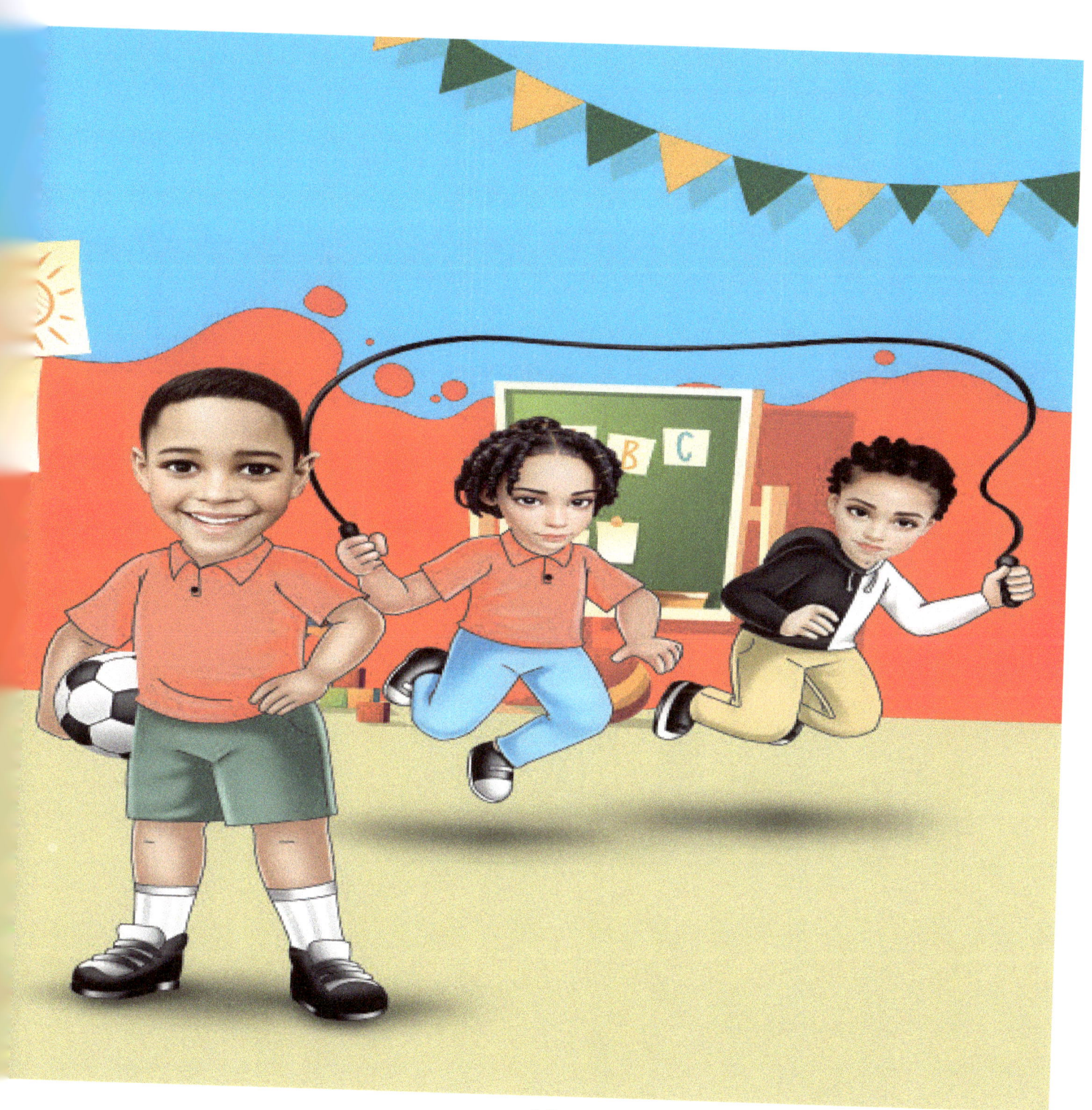

We took a few minutes to unwind by playing simon says, we had fun like we always do!

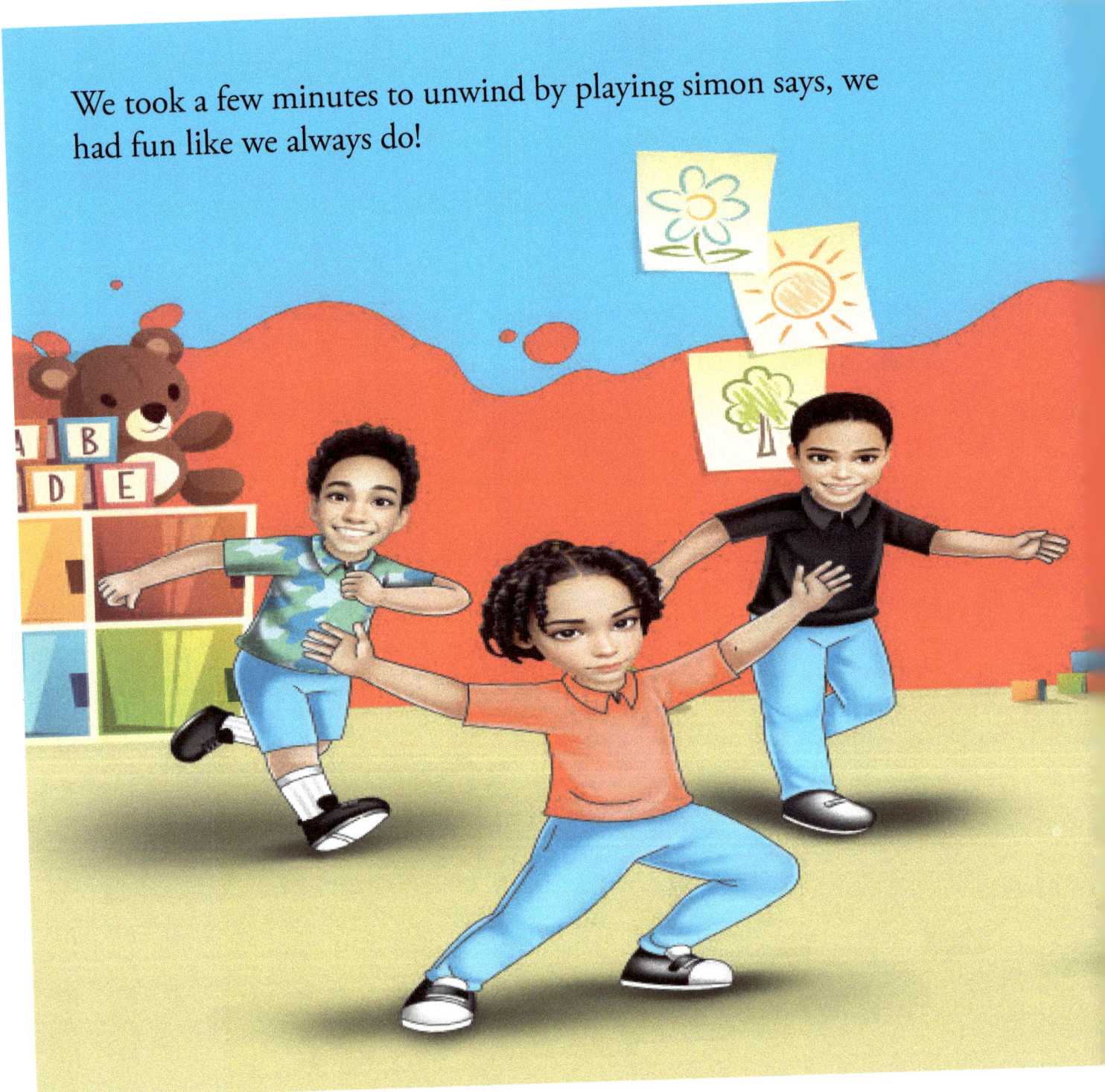

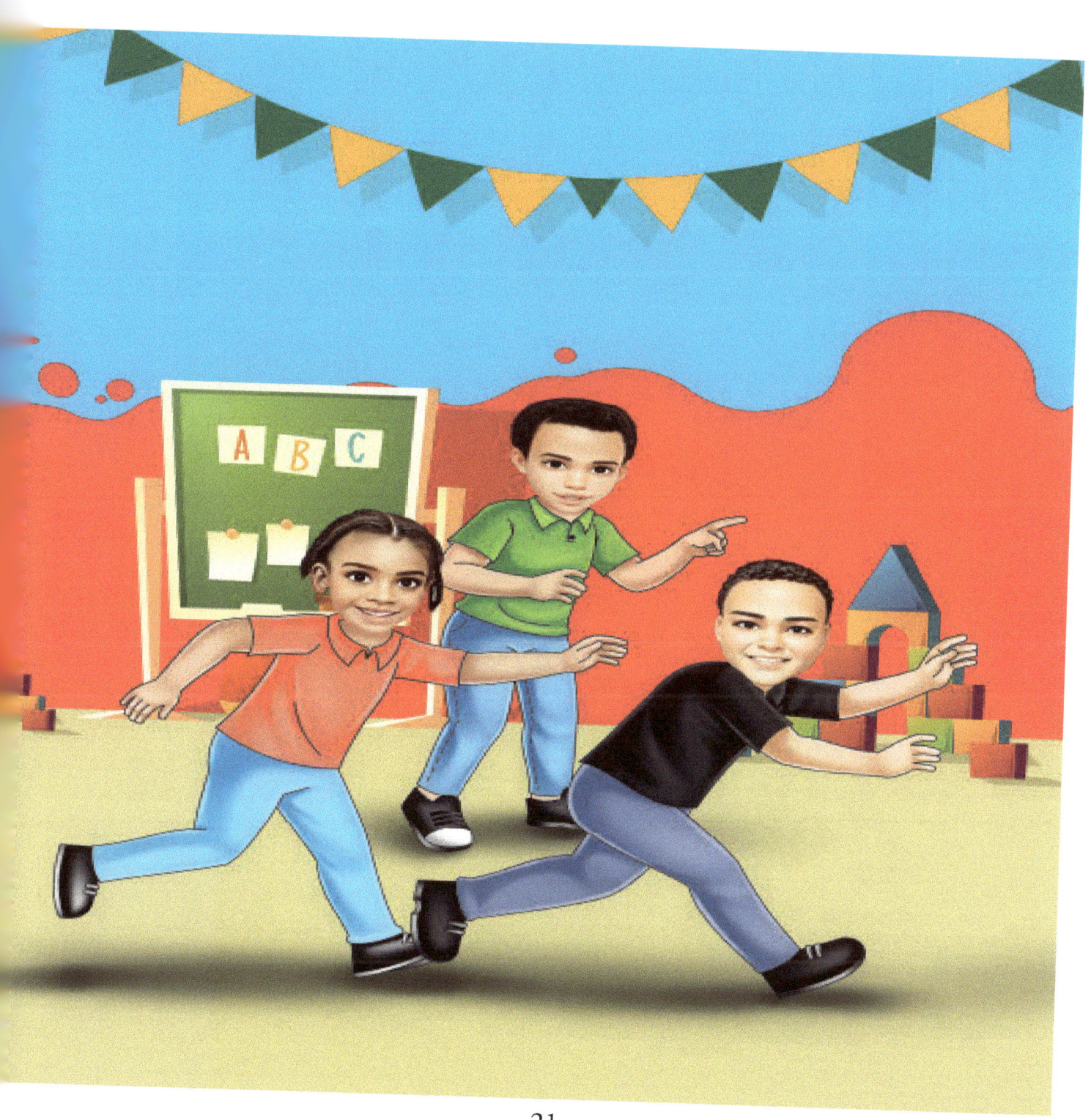

We couldn't wait for our parents to come and pick us up, so that they could see all the great work we did!

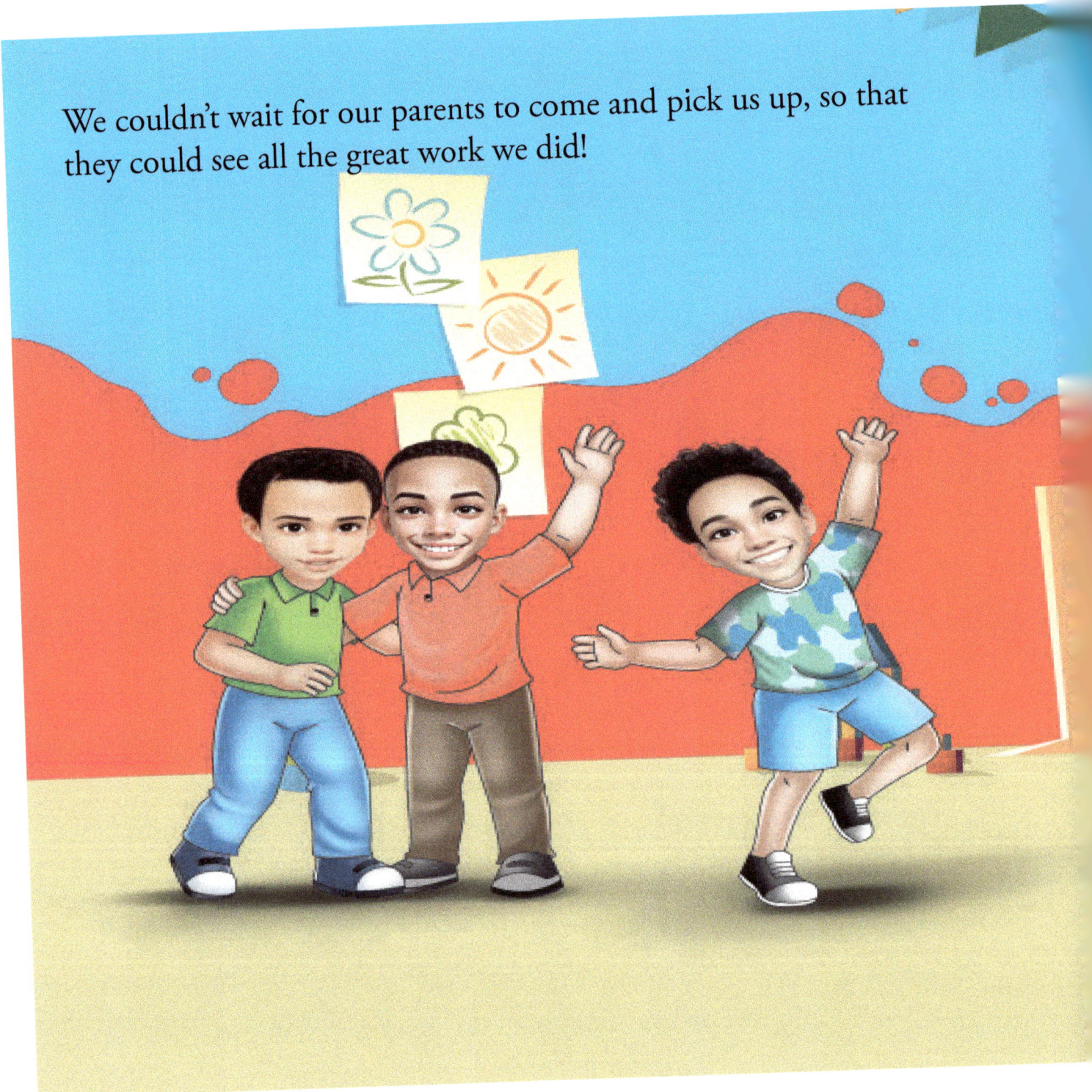

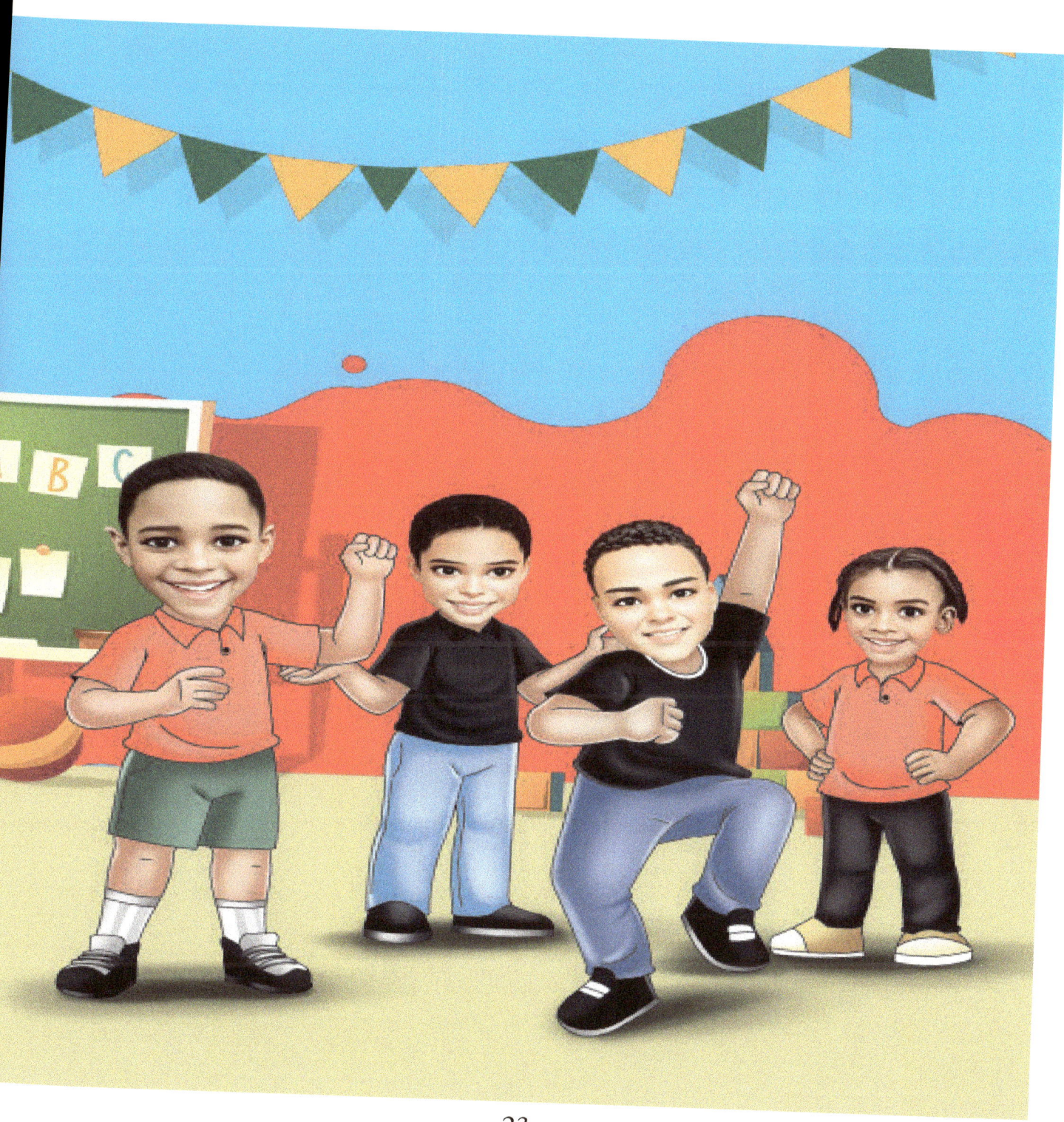

www.ingramcontent.com/pod-product-compliance
Lightning Source LLC
Chambersburg PA
CBHW040545220526
45473CB00016B/3026